THE FACEBOOK
BUSINESS SERIES

FACEBOOK

FOR BUSINESS SUCCESS

TOP SECRETS TO HELP YOU RUN A SUCCESSFUL BUSINESS ON FACEBOOK

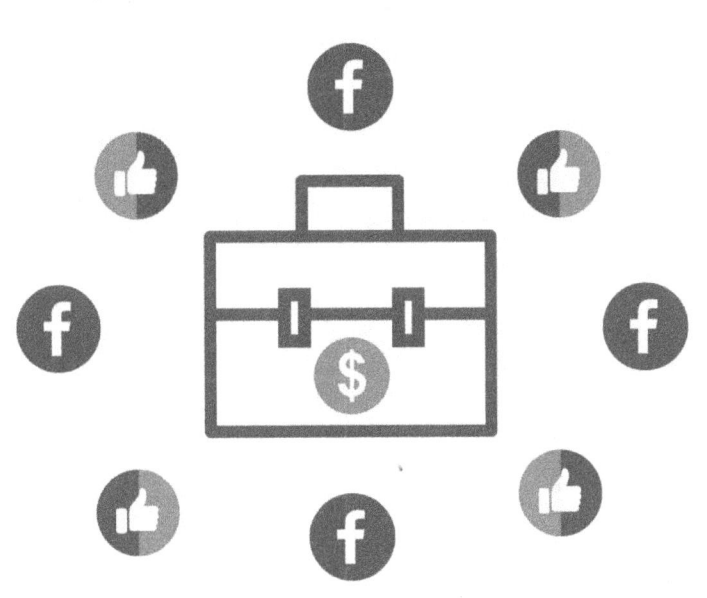

FACEBOOK FOR BUSINESS SUCCESS

Top Secrets to Help You Run a Successful Business on Facebook

Startup Jahswill

This book is part of the Facebook Business Series brought to you by StartUP Crest, a leading business development company with focus on startups and small businesses.

You can access more of our resources at

startupcrest.com

Take Your Business Online Facebook Group

Contact: info@startupcrest.com

+2348033867541

Table of Content

Introduction

Faccebook for Business Success

People are buying more products/services online due to the recommendations and promotions they come across on Facebook. A trend that won't die down any time soon.

To market your business successfully on Facebook, you need to understand Facebook's unique opportunities, and how it differs from other media. Just as you wouldn't run a radio jingle on television, you shouldn't market on Facebook the way you'd market in a newspaper or on your website.

Understand the Platform

Facebook EdgeRank

Did you know that not all your followers see your posts? Actually probably less than 16% of your followers see your page posts! Edgerank determines what posts appear on a Facebook user's newsfeed. The following factors are what Facebook uses to determine a post's Edgerank:

Affinity: Measures the relationship between the viewing user and the creator of the story. The closer the relationship between you, the higher the Affinity score. In other words, the more a follower interact with your post (and the more you interact with theirs) the higher the chances of them seeing your post.

Pro Tip: This is one reason why it is very important that you engage with your followers and their posts.

Weight: Different types of posts carry different weights (photos, videos, status updates, links, etc.). The higher the weight, the higher the score. Video tend to carry higher weight than photos and text in that order. Links seem to have the lowest weight score.

In recent times, Facebook, and all social media platforms gives a higher weight rating to **LIVE** posting.

Pro Tip: Here is one good reason you want to include live posting in your content strategy.

Time Decay: As a post ages it continually loses value. The quicker your followers engage with your content the better and higher score it will be assigned. What this means is that if two different pages share the same post at the same time, the one that people 'Like', 'Comment' and 'Share' first will have a higher Time Decay score.

Pro Tip: Encourage your employees, friends and business partners to engage with your post immediately you post it.

Page vs. Profile vs. Groups

Pages are for businesses and are entirely open to the public and search engines. Pages can also have applications and custom tabs to help engage with your audiences. You can have as many Pages as you want and there are no limits on the numbers of followers (likes) a page can have.

Profiles are for your personal use and represent you as a person. On your profile you have "friends". You are limited to 5000 friends and you're allowed to "like" or follow up to 500 pages. You're only allowed to have one personal profile on Facebook.

Groups are for people who share a common interest. Group members can participate in chats, upload photos to shared albums, collaborate on group documents and invite members who are friends to the group events. In Groups, there are 3 Privacy Options: Public, Closed or Private.

Facebook Terms of Service

Breaking Facebook rules may result in having your page/account banned without notice. Be familiar with the Facebook's Term of Service. Keep in mind that Facebook may change the TOS without notice. Visit Facebook to learn more https://www.facebook.com/policies.

Have a Clear Goal and Strategy

Determine what your goal(s) is for using Facebook. Using Facebook simply because the competition is, doesn't make an honest enough reason. Neither is it a good enough reason that I or some other pro says so.

It's important to have a clear goal for using Facebook, and a strategy to achieve that goal. For example, boutique might decide that its goal is to increase sales generated by Facebook by 20% in the next 3 months. Their strategy could include:

- creating a post every morning featuring a special offer of the day, using a coupon code so that the sale can be tracked to Facebook
- posting a daily photo featuring a customer who is its 'best dressed customer' of the day
- encouraging users to post their own photos of them looking cool in their products
- .Running a Facebook Lead generation app for 30 days to attract new customers.

Setting a goal and strategy gives you direction for your Facebook marketing and a way to measure your success.

Create Your Facebook Business Page

Creating a Facebook Page allows the more than 2 billion people on Facebook to discover your business – think of your Page as a digital storefront. Setting up a business Page is simple and free.

Two out of every 3 Facebook users across all countries say that they visit the Page of a local business at least once a week. Do you need any other motivation to create a Facebook page for your business?!

To start, you'll need to get your Page ready to go. Here are the steps you'll need to go through before we move into the finer details of your Facebook business strategy.

Setting up your Page

First of all, you'll need to actually set up your Facebook Page, if you haven't done so already.

For this, it's best to go directly to the source: Facebook itself has information on how to set up your business's Facebook Page, including a video tutorial. This step is very easy and should take you no more than 10 minutes to complete. Click here to go to Facebook page setup: https://web.facebook.com/business/pages/set-up?_rdc=1&_rdr

Add basic information

Don't even think about setting up your Page and leaving key areas blank! The first step to a successful Facebook business marketing strategy for your business is to make sure your Facebook Page itself is detailed and complete.

You'll want to do the following:

- Complete your "about" section
- During this step, you'll also select your unique url
- Upload a profile picture (could be any one of your storefront, product, logo, or something brand related)
- Add relevant information about your business such as opening hours, physical location(if you have an office where people can visit), and so on
- Create a cover photo (I use Canva for almost all my designs)
- etc

Tips to Setup a Professional Business Page

There are Facebook pages and there are "Facebook Pages." Some pages are just there. They're boring and they do nothing to attract their target audience. Other pages have the 'wow' factor. They're attractive, they provide great value and therefore the target audience is drawn in.

How do you ensure that your business page has that 'wow' factor? Let me show you:

Start With a Great Cover Photo

The image at the highest of your page can draw you in. It can capture your imagination and take you to some place beautiful. Show that you understand the importance of your cover photo which by using one which will work for you.

The image below will make for a great cover photo! Don't you agree?

Startups & Small Business Funding
How to quickly find business financing opportunities

Create a Profile Image That's Unique

When it involves profile pictures, we tend to use an image of ourselves up there and that's that. However, it is much more valueable in employing a unique profile image that your audience will remember . Start with defining what your business is about. Then attempt to create a picture that's memorable and creates strong branding. Pay a graphics editor if you would like to. It's worth it!

Make Use of the Facebook Page Apps

Facebook offers you some great apps, explore them and make use of it. Add any that are appropriate. Don't be afraid to use several ones. Apps such as Whatsapp Business can be very useful to drive conversations off Facebook.

Have a Strong Call to Action

It is vital that your Facebook page features a strong call to action, because without it your visitors won't know what they should do. Ask friends to click the 'LIKE', 'SHARE' or 'SIGNUP' button in a clear and concise way that leaves no room for mistakes.

At this point, your Facebook Page is functional and ready to go, although still pretty bare-bones. From here, you'll move on to actually creating unique posts for your Page, and onto creating a strategy to gain followers.

Create a Shorter Customized URL for Your Page

A shorter URL is straightforward for your visitors to recollect and it's easily promoted. See one of my pages short url: facebook.com/Startupjahswill. Simple an easy to remember!

Place Your 3 Most Important Tabs Next to the Photos Tab

This will make it easy for people who visit your page to quickly see what is most important about your page. This can easily drive engagement too.

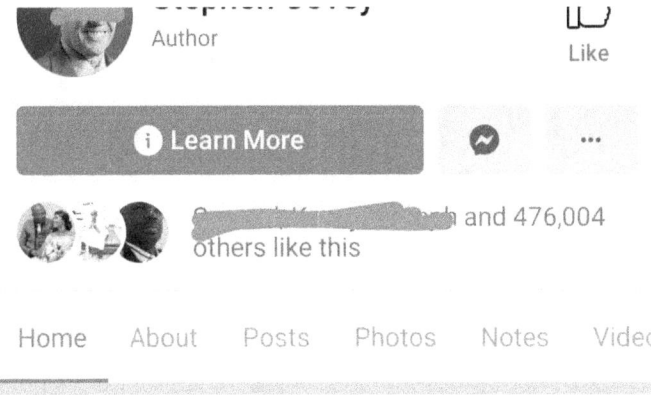

Identify Your Ideal Customer: Who is Your Target?

Have a clear idea of who you want to reach on Facebook. The more you know about them, the better you can target your message.

First, who is an ideal customer?

Answer: The person who really needs your products/services and are able to afford it right now or in the near future.

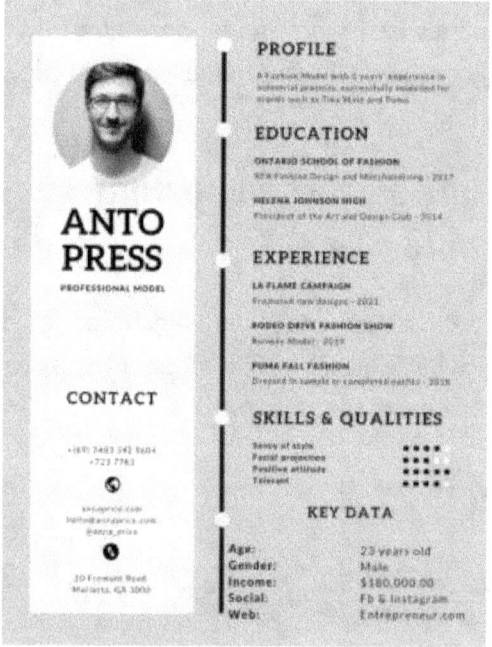

How do you identify that kind of person?

By creating a buyer persona. That is the profile of the kind of customer you want to do business with. Complete with their demographics, behavior online and offline and interests. Facebook makes this very easier with their "Audience Insights" tool.

I explained how to use this tool in detail in this video:

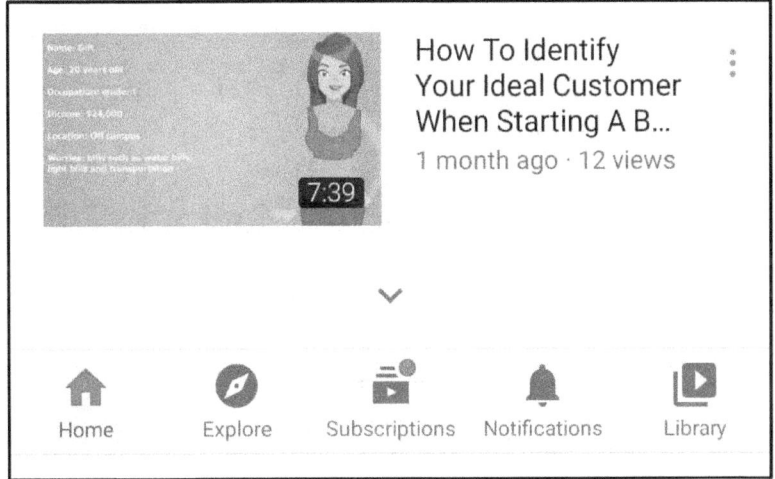

https://www.youtube.com/watch?v=oQacYq7RWDM

Click the link above to watch the video on Youtube and comeback here to continue.

Develop a Content Strategy

This is the important part: creating content that will resonate with your audience, help you gain new followers, and make them want to follow your Facebook Page and share what you post.

This section will be broken down into a few different subsections, as there is a lot to cover here.

Create a Mix of Different Types of Content

To an extent, what content you post will depend on what kind of business you're running.

Here are some types of content:

- Text (posts, blogs, articles, guides)
- Contests
- Announcements
- Live Videos
- Infographics
- Testimonials and reviews
- Electronic books (eBooks)
- Links to external content
- Images
- Videos
- Video Stories

Provide Valuable Content
What is Valuable Content?

Good content will play on life, living situations and interests of your target market. It is often associated with day-to-day life and will provoke a private response in the heart of your reader immediately. It relates to all or any sorts of content, asks for the opinion of users, and tells interesting stories.

Good content creates a community response where users gather to socialize and find something interesting to interact with people who share likes and interests.

If you're still unsure of the way to create good content, then have a glance at a number of the Facebook pages created and managed by large competitors in your industry. 'Copy' the type of content they are creating that resonates with your target customers.

You can create this type of content by defining your target market then determining what relevant topics are for that market. Then create themed content that you simply can schedule.

To make sure you're on track and getting the 'reach' you're after, you ought to use Facebook Page Analytics to research your posts. this will provide you with sound information which will allow you to be ready to observe decisions associated with your posts and future posts that you simply might make.

There are some ways you'll build your fan base that won't actually help your business prosper, so keep this in mind.

However, by taking the time to bring targeted traffic to your Facebook Page and growing a relevant fan base you'll enjoy the complete benefits of the work you set into this.

Long term your goal is to grow your follower base through 'Likes' and 'followers' and for them to like what you offer such that they tell their friends who will also tell their friends which can quickly grow, your business online.

To achieve this, you need to share content that people will really like and share. That will mean not always posting only about your offers.

The 80/20 rule will really benefit you here. Try publishing around 80% original and curated content that provides value to your followers and no more than 20% promotional content. Promotional content includes selling your products or services, posting about how great your customer find your business (unless your clients post it directly on your wall), showing your work or portfolio, promotion of your accomplishments, etc.

Relevant Content

Provide a mix of content related to your products or services. All too often we see Pages that post about random topics that are totally unrelated to their business. Don't stray too far off your topic!

What's In It for Your Customers?

Whenever you post to your page, remember that your page visitors want to know "what's in it for them". Be mindful of the content your post on your page to make sure you provide value to your visitors and followers. Most Facebook users Like pages to:

- Receive discounts or promotions
- Stay informed
- Get entertained
- Interact and connect
- Get Educated
- Show support

Your content should cater to all those needs from time to time.

Secrets to Engage Your Customers

Facebook is a social network platform for conversation. On your Facebook Page are you talking to your followers or chatting with them? A good indicator is the number of followers you have. If you want more followers than you have, then it's time to make some changes.

To get the most out of your page you need to understand your 'social space.' On Facebook there needs to be a lot of conversing back and forth to share information. This includes photos, links, videos and posts.

Here are 7 fail proof secrets to make sure you get it right.

1. Provide Useful and Interesting Content

In addition to offering free things or coupons confirm that the content that's on your page is beneficial, interesting and enticing . That way your visitors are more likely to comment and strike up a conversation. In turn, those conversations get shared which spreads your reach.

2. Invite a Few of Others Help Manage Your Page

These people will create content and also engage with your followers. They will also suggest it to their friends and your reach can grow. Additionally , having more than one page administrator offers different perspectives, which may help to make the page interesting. It also can make responding to posts and comments more efficient. As your page grows, the more admins you ought to consider having.

3. Encourage Your Visitors to Post Pictures on Your Wall

Facebook users love pictures, so cash in on this and encourage your followers to openly share their photos.

4. Post Inspirational Images

Inspirational images are always well received. In fact, they're among the foremost popularly shared posts on Facebook. So make sure to incorporate them on your Facebook Page. Your followers will be moved to share and comment.

5. Use Contests and Sweepstakes

It's very easy to run a contest or sweepstakes on Facebook. You'll may even require that Facebook participants like your page before being allowed to participate. This will not only increase engagement but also likes and followers.

Pro Tip: This can really increase your fans/likes. However, many businesses set about this the incorrect way. They promote their competition using Newsfeeds. You ought to not do that because it's against Facebook's terms & conditions. Run your contest properly using an app like Wildfire or Strutta. There are variety of other contest apps you'll can use.

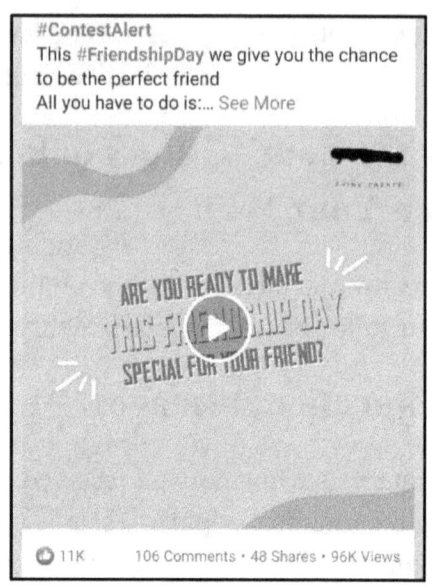

Common sorts of contest include video or photo submissions. This contest and sweepstake work best once you have over 500 likes and followers.

6. Reply Promptly to Comments/Posts

Replying promptly to any posts is additionally very important. The faster you're to replying to your followers the more likely that they're going to still engage you.

When someone likes or comment on a post you want to reply to their comment. Ideally, what you would like to realize is conversation that goes back and forth between you and your followers is counted as engagement by Facebook.

By allowing your followers to feel a conversation is happening they're more likely to participate. This encourages other followers to also engage with your posts.

If you post and a follower comments and you don't reply the conversation dies off and therefore the reach dies with it.

7. Ask Your Followers for Their Opinion

Never underestimate the power of asking. 'What's your opinion?', 'Why do you think so and so"? For instance, once you post links from experts, especially 'hot topics' or controversial topics, ask your audience for his or her opinion, their feedback. Your goal is to get conversation together with your fans and to bring new followers on board.

Secrets to Creating Facebook Posts That Are Engaging

If you would like to grow your followers base and increase your likes, you will have to share posts to your page that are interesting and keep your visitors eager to return.

Here are 8 Secrets to create Facebook posts that are engaging.

1. Use Copy, Images and Videos That Are Engaging

- Photos and videos that are media rich will get attention and that they will help your message be more noticeable on a News feed
- Lifestyle and inspirational images are always engaging. Smart Page owners are quick to require advantage of those images, because they understand they are doing not need to be relevant to the product/service you offer to be relevant to your fans. These fans will then share these posts with their friends which provides you with more reach and another opportunity to grow your 'Likes'
- Share images/photos of your products together with your customers enjoying them

Pro Tip: The best text –based posts are between 100 and 250 words long. Anything longer than that may not be read to the end by your audience.

2. Create Content That's Shareable

Good content is great, but great content is much better. It's vital to possess content that's shareable. This suggests your content is so good that your audience doesn't just want to love it, they need to share it with their own friends. The content that your followers share is basically a part of their online identity. It tells others what they like and who they're. You want to make sure that your posts are things they can be proud of!

When content is shareable, it increases your posts like because it exposes your name to more people, putting your brand out there ahead of these that aren't currently your followers.

3. Post Fresh and Trending Topics

When your posts are associated with what they're thinking about at the time, like holidays or a current sporting event, your audience is far more likely to interact.

4. Share Lots of Photos and Videos

People prefer photos over texts. Make your Facebook Page visually appealing using graphics, photos and videos. This may draw the interest of your followers and that they are far more likely to share photos, graphics and videos than text, which successively extends your reach.

5. Post Regularly

The world is fast-paced and constantly changing. Your Facebook activity needs to move at that speed. If you want to keep your followers engaged, then you must constantly share fresh content and be consistent. On today, off tomorrow will not work on Facebook. They will quickly forget about you and move on!

Your Facebook posts are time and date stamped. Your posts are grouped monthly so your fans can easily scroll down your page and that they also can see how often you post. So if you simply post 7 times over the weekend then not again until subsequent weekend your followers will lose interest and new potential followers aren't getting to be too excited about liking your page.

6. Post Interesting Stuffs

Posts don't need to be news to be interesting. Your fans aren't getting to have an interest in news unless it's relevant, but they could have an interest in learning a few new products that's coming. Plug that to what's relevant for your business.

7. Watch Your Post Timing

If you would like the the highest number of people to engage with your posts, then you would like to post when most of the people are on Facebook. Generally mornings and afternoons are best, but in fact you've got to determine what's best for your audience. Use the Insight tool to find out this information.

Pro Tip: If you don't have a large following yet that wil guide your decision, 'spy' on the competition. When are they posting mostly? Which times do they have the highest engagement?

8. Don't Only Promote, Share

Your Facebook Page doesn't exist just to plug your products/services. If that's all you are doing with it, your followers will lose interest quickly. Use your Page to urge people interested that might make use of your products/services to interact and socialize.

Proven Secrets to Increase Your Page Likes

Your followers are the core to your Facebook Page being successful. But building those fans and

'Likes' are often quite challenging!

Let's check out 7 secrets to grow your Facebook Page likes:

1. Take Advantage of Offline Public Events

Often overlooked, yet a strong tool which will be an excellent opportunity to spread the word. If you have a public speaking gig for instance, make certain you include your Facebook Page URL on the slide show because it makes it easy for people to see. If you attend networking meetings this is often an excellent time to encourage members to 'Like' your Facebook Page and become followers.

2. Encourage Check-Ins on Your Facebook Page

For anyone who features a brick and mortar business, you ought to enable check-ins on your Facebook page, then remind customers to check-in once they are in your business premises. You might even include an incentive like offering a bonus for those who participate .

3. Followers Fridays

On Facebook, there are Pages that host Followers Friday events. If you're participating, you'll be encouraged to present either a video or text post. Use that opportunity to introduce your business to everyone that's participating then tag your page within the post.

Pro Tip: Taking this to the next level, run through all the comments and 'Like' each of the participating pages who will in turn 'Like' your page.

Pro Tip: A word of caution. Only participate in local events because if you finish up with plenty of international followers, it could actually lower your EdgeRank score. Additionally , if others hide your news feed posts because they only wanted the 'Like' from you and aren't curious about your business, could hurt you.

4. Make Use of Your Business Signage

When customers visit your brick and mortar business, you can have a signage in your storefront that encourages customers to 'Like" your page.

5. Use Other Social Media

The use of social media channels like LinkedIn, Google+ or Twitter are an excellent avenues to encourage people to go to your Facebook page. These are free marketing tools that you simply should cash in on. Additionally, ensure that you sometimes occasionally cross post from one to the opposite .

6. Grow Your Facebook Fans and Likes With Contests

This is one among the simplest methods to excite people about your page and to draw new followers to your page. The lure of winning the large prize means your target market goes all the way to 'click Like,' and become a follower on your page.

7. Invite Facebook Friends to Like Your Page

You can really give your follower base a lift by simply asking your friends to 'Like' your page.

Best kept Secrets to Increase Your Posts Reach

If you would like more Facebook followers then you want to ensuure your page is as visible as you possibly can make it to a relevant audience.

Here are 7 Proven Secrets to Help You Do That

1. Use the Business Pages of Others

If you're a brick and mortar business, you ought to 'Like' other local businesses page. Make comments on their pages as your page not your personal name. If you discuss posts where others have already commented, depending on what their privacy settings are, they're going to be notified that you posted making you get increased visibility.

2. From Your Personal Profile Add a Link to Your Business Page

Use your personal profile to feature a link to your business page. A number of your friends will find what you are doing useful. You'll even mention your own page in your status updates now and then to encourage friends to go to your Page and if they like what you've got to supply , they could click the 'Like' button and grow your followers.

3. Tag Yourself in Your Photos

This technique is very easy to use that you'll wonder why you didn't use it sooner. From now on every single photo that you post on your Facebook Page confirm that you tag yourself in every single photo. This is often smart because if your content is sweet and its shareable then it'll appear on the news feeds of others. When one among your followers shares it, then it's getting to be linked within the 'shared section' additionally to the image your follower shared.

4. Use Engagement Ads

Most marketers use Facebook adverts solely to encourage users to buy something. Using engagement ads to build your following can yield longterm benefits too. Engagement ads are different because they aim to plug your Facebook Page rather promoting the sale of a particular product.

5. Get Your Existing Followerss to Share Your Page Content

Your current followers are key to your building your follower base and watching it grow. Once you publish relevant content on your page, your existing followers are more likely to share that material which can cause new followers finding your page, thanks to their posts.

So, don't be shy? Ask your followers to share your posts to reach more people. Also, posting regularly valuable content helps to encourage your followers to share the content you post.

6. Other Marketing Sources

Add your Facebook URL to all of your marketing opportunities such as letterhead, business cards, brochures, etc. Make sure that you use a customized Facebook URL for your page, because the assigned URLs are long and ugly.

7. Make Sure You Offer Valuable Content

If you want your followerss to visit your page often and share it, then you need to make sure you offer content that's of value. If you consistently provide top-notch content, your follower base will grow as your reach grows.

In addition to that, the first time someone finds your page they'll like what they see and want to read more of what you have to offer and so they are much more likely to 'Like' your page.

Using Facebook Ads to Boost Your Business

One of the simplest ways to extend your Facebook likes is thru the utilization of Facebook Ads, which permit you to focus on specific demographics, which suggests it'll allow you to bring the traffic you desire to your page.

Do not confuse Facebook Ads with Google Ads, because they're not an equivalent . Google Ads will show up when an individual actively searches keyword(s) you pre-identified. They are actively searching for what you are selling and will most likely click your ads if they are relevant.

Facebook Ads on the other hand don't work that way. A Facebook Ad shows up when an individual is browsing their News Feed. What it means is that they likely don't have any intent to buy from you at that point. That will mean you want to offer incentives to drive clicks on the Facebook Ad using something that the user desires.

Therefore, you may have ads like the following:

* Like us and obtain your Free Guide to Growing Your Instagram likes

* Like us to get 10% on your next purchase with us

* Like us to win a free Marketing Consultation

Facebook Ads also are far more affordable than Google Ads. Meaning even if you've got a really low budget you can still take advantage of Facebook Ads.

What Next for You?

Now you have been shown the best kept secrets of running a successful business on Facebook! What next for you? Are you going to sit on a long thing or take action to start growing your business today?

I understand some people may want more, like a one-on-one guidance. That's why for a limited time, I will be making myself available to guide you if you need more help with your Facebook business or selling online generally.

Just send me an email at info@startupcrest.com let's talk about how best to support you further.

About the Author

StartUP Jahswill

Entrepreneur | Public Speaker | Online Business Coach

Eduzobe Jahswill Udogbo (StartUP Jahswill) is a trained Physicist with a passion for building and growing small businesses.

He is the CEO of StartUP Crest, a company he formed to help young people start and grow small businesses. He is also the CEO of LabHub Medical Laboratories and Diagnostics and the founding Managing Partner/General Manager of Karone Photo World Ltd, both very successful startups.

In 2009 he setup his first registered company, SwiftTech Integrated Solutions Ltd with the aim of providing alternative power supply to residents of the satellite towns around the Nigerian capital territory, Abuja.

Although that venture turned out to be a total failure, Jahswill learned valuable lessons that have helped him to start and grow other businesses with varied degrees of success.

His number one desire is to help as many young people as possible to discover their entrepreneurial skills and use this to start and grow businesses that will provide employment and livelihood.

His mission is simple: help young people transition from frustrated job seekers and disillusioned startups to successful entrepreneurs.

He promotes financial education that helps young people understand the career options available to them as a means of creating wealth as opposed to the old one-way thinking of "Go to School, get a good job and live comfortably ever after"!

Jahswill appreciates that while university/college education might be a necessity in some chosen careers, it is just one of the options and not the surest path to creating wealth. That is why he advocates learning business and financial skills that gives the best and surest path to wealth creation. He spends most of his time developing content for his various educational platforms especially his blog www.startupcrest.com where he provides valuable resources for startups.

He is happily married and blessed with a beautiful daughter.

Other Books by the Author!

*No Bullshit Business Plan: *How to Write a Business Plan Easily and Convincingly*

*Facebook Marketing Mistakes: *14 Newbies Mistakes that are Holding Your business Down*

*Facebook Posts Engagement Secrets: *20 Proven Strategies to Get More Likes, Comments and Shares on Your Facebook Post*

*Social Media Content to Cash: *Easily Create Content for Social Media (And Make Money from Your Content)*

*Take Your Business Online: *The Step-by-Step Guide to Taking Your Offline Business Online (Even if You Have No Tech Knowledge)*

Click Here to Get a Copy